**There Will Be
No Miracles Here**
Stephen Sawyer

Smokestack Books
1 Lake Terrace, Grewelthorpe, Ripon HG4 3BU
e-mail: info@smokestack-books.co.uk
www.smokestack-books.co.uk

ISBN 9781999827601

Smokestack Books
is represented
by Inpress Ltd

*To Dad, Mum
and brother Phillip*

# Contents

Orgreave Mass Picnic                                            9
Picasso's Bull                                                 16
Draft for the Contemporary Love Poem                           17
Time Served                                                    21
Central Lending                                                23
Niobe of Gaza                                                  25
The Wedding Song of Whirlow Park                               27
Eyewitness                                                     30
The Iron Woman                                                 31
Six Goodbyes of the Eightfold Path                             33
Nostalgia for the Light                                        38
The Laughter of Women                                          40
Ithaca                                                         41
Afterlife                                                      43
How Long                                                       45
Chute                                                          46
Dark Matter                                                    49
Litany                                                         51
Flood                                                          54
Host Rufus Regardless Addresses the Artists at Dr Sketchy's    59
Classically Trained                                            61
Permit                                                         62
In Search of Yellow House Lane                                 63
Do I Still Exist If You Don't See Me?                          64
Oak                                                            66
Memoir                                                         68
This Lightening Never Ends                                     73
Meeting Marx in the Sheaf View                                 74
There Will Be No Miracles Here                                 75
Untitled                                                       78

Notes                                                          79
Acknowledgements                                               83

# Orgreave Mass Picnic

I

I'm walking with friends
between acoustic tent and main stage,
in lush fields, where the Battle
of Orgreave took place.

Remember who's drawing warships
at the back of the class
while the 'A' kids learn maths;
cast as the turnspit 'jailer'
of Antonio, wearing sackcloth
in the service of Shylock;
a metallic silver-painted sword
for a part without a word.

You could confuse Zulu drum
– beats of truncheons on shields
with the echo of speakers
in these fields: a Sex Pistols
tribute band, scissor-kicking
in drainpipe black, a bearded man
in a red t-shirt: *Keep Calm
and Read Marx.*

## II

Sitting with miners in Beighton Welfare
waiting for the picket call
then hands are braced
against van roofs as we hurtle
in convoy across barrens
that look like a mace-dented breastplate
under a faint rind of moon.
A light floats to the surface – blinks,
a string-vested man sings
at a frosted bathroom window:
*I left my heart in San Francisco.*

Kiveton Park our destination,
where a gas explosion kills nine men,
miners build the listed baths
and the pit yard sings to the village
over the diverted tannoy:
*San Quentin, you've been livin' hell
to me ... Goodnight Sweetie ... at 58,
Nettleham Road ... Goodnight Sweetie*

A nacreous arc bisects our route,
down to third, a bandaged tree,
second, *Laundry Works,*
missing letters & Sons,
*Butchers Entrance*, time
out of joint, back up to third –
and a backward glance:
child ghosts, a grim reaper,
painted on boarded up windows;
a cooker lit by its own irony
on forecourt ruins
and we're flying again
in the lung-dust darkness.

The colliery's beaming eyes clock
you like a head wound, frame
versions of winding towers,
and pit baths, silhouette coppers
with dogs, patrolling the grounds
like hired guns from out of town.


Kettled and pushing back, a flask
flying: a single scorpion shadow
in the marsh window light
of a colliery bus as it crosses the line.


### III

This is a reconstruction:

A cattle baron refused the free run
of ploughed land, hires a gunfighter
as mean as a scabbard with eyes
to clear the homesteaders off.

A beleaguered farmer slogs
through the wagon-rutted mud,
reaches the saloon porch where
the assassin, Frank Wilson, smile
drawn tight as a vultures talons,
closes the angle on higher ground.

*One Arthur Scargill*
*There's only one Arthur Scargill*
A shirtless kid leaps over flowers
in neighbourhood gardens,
mounted police galloping full-tilt
tearing them up, behead the sun.

## IV

People I haven't seen since the strike
greeting me on the battle site
where the miners fought to stop
the flow of coal in and out
of the now absent coking plants.
Compere, Attila-the-Stockbroker
rises above a failed microphone,
leaps off-stage into the crowd to bray
and snort his narrative poem
of class lore home. A man, naked
from the waist up, lying face down
and left for dead. A woman sitting
in a deck chair picking up a stitch.


## V

Women of the communal kitchen
insist I eat a free dinner
though I'm not a miner on strike.

Mums, Dads and kids, playing
with tennis ball and dustbin lid
on summer evenings. *You know
she sold her wedding ring to pay
the lecky bill?* Can you hear
the pit yard sing: *Ol' Man River?*

Pensioners legless on elderflower
falling over sequestered pews
along the candlelit terraces
at the anti-Princess Di festivities.
Can you hear the pit yard sing?
*And did those feet in ancient times…*

Three hours baby-sitting
for a sack of beetroot. Eight pints
of homebrew for fixing an engine.
Sheer weight of numbers
beating off bailiffs. Can you hear
the pit yard sing: *The miners united,*
*will never be defeated*?


## VI

I return to myself as the feet
of this kid, the hands of that kid,
others who are myself, running
for the ball in a shell suit of fog.
A bear chases the Avon Lady.
*Wanna buy a chamois leather?*
The Avon Lady chases a bear.

Laughter in the cage ascending
at 25 feet per second, stomachs
leaping as the sun sets fire
to the tongues of those who harvest
the hard fruit of the deep earth,
inseparable from saltpetre, water,
and forebears, who are themselves.
Can you hear the pit yard sing?
*We're sold, solid as a rock.*

That way of hanging out, power
of the untamed thought
between chimney pots, chinks
of curtain light, bits of motor bike,
a mother's valium lips, thinking
without banister rails. A first love,

a mirage's sister, receding
as I approach her Bacall-glam eyes,
and braced front teeth, who
always got a speaking part.
Her mind I knew like the Sea
of Tranquillity, tried to find
one Sunday, amidst verandas
of blue hydrangeas; the absences
of abstract sculptures, a Pekinese
cradled in arms, garden walls
of slab-cut lumber; a union jack;
the Spion kop chanting of a train,
calling me back, calling me back.


## VII


Pears and carnation milk for tea
Harry Secombe's flaccid grin
on *Songs of Praise*
but my dad said he could sing –
*Love is a Many-Splendored Thing* –
streets you enter your life in, meet

Shane, the kid who loves
the eponymous western, starring
Alan Ladd; goes to his surface job
at the colliery in his Stetson hat
with spurs strapped on his boots –
shepherded and supported
by the miners. Tea breaks, you
find him perfecting his quick draw,
six-gun hanging from his holster,
girlfriend with flask and snap.

A foreman told to address *the problem*
suggests 'the lass' take herself off –
*Cook for yah man at 'ome.*
Shane centres his balance,
draws on his irons, squeezes
the trigger, releasing the hammer
on a roll of percussion caps:
*Git yah hands off a ma' woman* –
a perfect Missouri drawl.


## VIII

Children release balloons
in front of the main stage.
All the time of light
and a hiss of anger remain
in the green apple I bite into.

Pit-boot flush in stirrup-cup, Shane
hoists himself up. A sparrow hawk
circles the listed baths. His woman
holding and held, swinging aboard
to laughter and applause of admin
and canteen. I canter on my heart.

# Picasso's Bull

This bull, made of nitrates and onions
from the veins of the earth. Pyrenees
under pelt; skin, tight and ticking,
a grandfather clock, a flutter
of goldfinch, a bald man turning his
back, on a bald man turning his back –
tattoo on his armpit; a tumult
of face flesh dragging on fastenings:
bloodshot orbs, almost eyeless.

Stripping down – lines, tones, styles –
wanting less than a shrug of the scruff.
This bull escapes itself, returning half-
human, rivet-stitched, armour-plated,
a winged minotaur of immolation.

He is a boy playing blind man's bluff
by a dried oak-stump before the attack
and he's not wearing a shirt.

Throwing out the bell and rosette art
history, with nothing left over; self-
possessed in emptiness, incubating
death's deceit, he walks towards you.

# Draft for the Contemporary Love Poem

*after Tadeusz Różewicz*

You've got to be quick
to describe a horse;
within seconds
it becomes another horse
or an unknown painter's horse
and then its human face appears;
it finds time for sarcasm,
places a rose at your feet.

A hand can be described,
through a palm and fingers
that become a fist, a mouth
you have kissed by a tree
that has no final shape;
in it are twisting distances,
a trust in water
and the sun's first ray.

In the past, love poems
described mossiness,
a rector's existential doubt,
a dove-keeper's eternal pant,
or the other way round.

Eyelids are described
through tree roots. Whiteness
by a gable end silhouette
jacketed in scaffolding,
a minor chord of roosting birds
on the telegraph wires.

A springlike description of love
is a bud of green thought
that questions the meaning
of flowering trees.

The ankles and thighs
of Juliet Ms Muse, surrender
an upside-down hold.
Her shoulder folding
on stage, bearing the weight
of her arcing spine
as if she's tilting out
of the Horsehead Nebula
of her own mind's fire:
an apt description
of a crucified passion
if you know nothing
about dancing pole.

A practical description of love
is the discernible hands
of an ancestor, under-coating
white shutters, high ceilings
and sash windows.

A telling description
of the swelling breast
includes the solid planting
of the forward hooves.
I wheel him away:
he bears me full circle
head jerking, neck – a tower
of exalted salt.

I who am alive, begin again
stuck on the pin of a word,
wanting to embrace the dark
like a mouth in a wound,
inhale the fetid vapours
till my cheeks swell, nostrils
dilate and lips compress.
I hardly know how to undress.

Some things take you closer
to your life. The talent
and luck to describe a horse
that leaps out of a poem
to bear you on. Eyes that fill
underwater worlds, raise you
to the surface, resuscitate
your soul. The gap between
teeth and tongue, a hand
in the dark, shadow without
shadow, light without light.

A body describing the desire
of a body in a thousand forests
of sleep. Juliet Ms Muse,
more than herself and the illness
of hope, in each shift
of emphasis and feat of strength.

You have to be quick
to describe a cloud;
within seconds
it becomes bread, a sky without
sky; nuzzling elephants
drunk on sweet marula fruit,
collapsed in a heap.

A crackle of rain, a voice
down the line…
telling you to buy birdseed,
asking you if you're eating.

The black bird in my cypress
who listens, sings to an echo
that questions an echo
of the contemporary love poem.

# Time Served

I watched you chop and flip the mortar,
shuffle a deck of cards. The veins stood out,
highways in your arms. I wanted to swing
the hammer, hear its voice descend the scale
to stammer a blunt-thud when the nailhead
was flush. Slice off wafers of tawny timber
that quivered in figures of six on the face
of the plane. I wanted to rag-dab
on the knotting, stem the flow of resin, seal;
sand the wood, prime – with milk-thin paint.
You barely had time to mortise and tenon
crossbar and upright before I was a brother
of the brush and the cat, a silhouette,
on the corrugated roof of the motorbike shed.
You and the 'know-how' of builder's yard,
taproom, tool shed – against the homilies
of that post-war nation, bolting itself together,
like a brylcreemed Frankenstein in denim
while your trowel was salmon, flashing
on our gable end; Petula Clarke's, *Down Town*
on a radio that beat itself up between stations
without constant attention.  I made a kind
of sense of the Bay of Pigs, knew whose side
you were on: apple trees, pigeon lofts, time-
served workers, a ladder to the sky.
I first read John Pilger's exclusive dispatches
from butchered Phnom Penh in your *Mirror*.

You, half a teaspoon of sugar and a blowlamp
in a pram. Steptoe and Son, Till Death Us
Do Part, our exploding TV. I wanted to pour
liquid gloss through a sieve of nylon stocking.
You and the art of stirring flour and soda
into a bucket of boiling water. Bobby Charlton
checking, inversing the line of attack, wrong
-footing Franz Beckenbaur, pubic school voice
Ken Wolstenholme, our grainy black and white
front room: *Some people are on the pitch;*
*they think it's all over.*

Paintbrushes, now fifty years old, still stand
in cans, sable stocks below the waterline, at all
times; plash of turpentine to keep the bristles
in fettle. I sit, look at canhooks, twofoots;
a plumbob that says if the world is on the level.

# Central Lending

Yesterday morning I'm at the keys
in Central Lending when I hear the ripped vowel
of a seagull's cry over calm water.

I look around the table, see a young woman
the colour of rosewood, tears of barley pearl,
her cheeks diffusing the light of hot flesh.

Users of the computer suite are staring at her
and one another, as if she were flailing her limbs
like ocean-rich kelp or conjuring a marmoset
from her tunic sleeve. Keyboards of the People's
Network, clack. A hole-punch bolts a perfect 'O'.
Spectacles ride smiles and a bracelet leaps
on a wrist by the One-Week-Loan Best-Sellers.

A sharp intake of breath breaks into sobbing –
like the last half-dozen strokes of a saw blade
ascending the scale before it draws on air.
Strangely, I anticipate it; need it more
than I need a Patagonian llama to shamble
through this library door *en route* for Music and Film.

The people round the table stare at me now
as well as her, as if she and I were one.
Vowels drift like dandelion seeds to fade
between Poetry and Adventure. I go to her:
scalded eyes like mineral springs, disbelieving,
the hot liquid sluicing through her eye lashes;
the crackle of leather around a shoulder,
under an arm, as someone reaches for a key.

I return to my seat, nodding assuredly
like a dashboard dog. Ker-ching! A fine paid.
Clunk! A date stamped. A lion is killing a gazelle
on the monitor to my left; the girl's arms waving
at counter-staff, tears like melting rouge
on her face; her SOS turning to jubilation:
*It's OK, I've done it – it's OK! Thank you
so much.* Laughter round the table, a tower
of birds in a basement of books.

I want to give her my apple fritter, to celebrate
these moments that contain her happiness
and what the day will bring –
but I am dancing with the tigress in the sun.

# Niobe of Gaza

She sees her children in the open pores
of sunset as bluish purple flowers
on a high-rise balcony washing-line full,
as swaying blue jeans, a table of crayons,
a girl's blouse concealing an alarm clock
that faintly rings in a world where truth
is a bundle of wet kindling.

> She sees her children
> in the blown ash
> of a side board, a neck tie,
> a brittle white school shirt,
> a row of empty desks.

Should she write:
Please Help children missing, last seen
in classrooms, chalk dust, making fun
of the mad village poet, selling courgettes
in the souk. A poster for every clinic,
village square and yard of separation wall,
written in the unsubmissive spirit of the olive.

> Where is this street
> they have hidden from her?
> The House of Waiting Bowls: 48 pieces
> of fine china and a haunted kettle.
> The smell of cooking stew, stronger
> than the power of revolutionary phrases.
> Dolls made of soft leaves, branches
> and paper, a carton of caterpillars
> under the dining room table.

She passes through them, a semi stranger,
a semi sentence, a semi rhythm, a semi
arrival and departure under cover
of darkness, a semi relocation. They pass
through her in a breeze of sleep,
swinging round military watchtowers
writing martyrs' names on a piece of sun.

What act of forgiveness
could she train herself to perform?
Her enemy gods haunted and cursed
bang on the night's ceiling with a cane.

She sees her children carried
on a wave of palms and victory signs,
so many lost in thought
as if they know death is more alive than we think.

Do they know her. Is she, she –
with broken spectacles,
they have not watched her hair turn grey.
Does she remember the spreading fig tree
that fed the generations, 49 widows,
then left to litter the square with fruit.
Does she know they cut it down ?

# The Wedding Song of Whirlow Park

*Dad, come on dad, come on mum – run.*
What a shock to realise that I was this 'dad'
– a woman calling, waving – on the lawn
facing the oblong forecourt at the front
of the estate, where I'd been sitting
on a park-bench, dedicated to the memory
of A Giant of a Dog, as the chrome grilles
and cream tail-fins of the stretch-limousines
oozed-up the gravel drive like hammerhead sharks.
Then, from the side of the house, the men
in frockcoats, swallows drinking in flight;
women, hand-signing for a draw
on a shared cigarette: low v-line necks
and butterscotch calves, dresses of gold
and lavender, sleeveless and purple, ruby
and strapless. One: ivory, mermaid tight,
thighs of nude pink in the sunshine.

It must have been the timbre of her voice:
*Dad – come on!* Such a tender imperative
that lit that sense that I was 'him' – this 'dad',
who's standing next to me – and that 'we'
were 'they', this whirlpool of tree ferns
and caspia, pink candles and lumps of butter,
soft, wide-brimmed black hats at 26 degrees.
Why don't they just ask me to leave?
I'm not one of them; I'm older and younger,
louder when vulgar; mostly, say nothing
at all. Photographs! Caught – writing my
escape, a dog bowl of stagnant water
at my feet. The serrated skyline
of marching pines with associating blues,
greens and variegated shading, bordering
the lawns. Ponds that teem with water fowl,
reflect yellow fleeces of laburnum that break up,

come together. I feel I know these guests
I haven't met: iron-bridge direct, vowels
hammer-bounced flat for a tang; that roar
of the earth, let-me-begin-again laughter.

I stare into the baize-green, mid-distance,
the little helpers, holding the bridal train
above rolling lawns, the married couple
ascending flights of steps, thumbs-up
to applause; one woman – I return
to this one woman – cropped, dark hair;
a pink-mauve gown, with halter neck,
a pulse of sadness in her chanting eyes,
her smoker's husky laughter, scratched
and dry, buffed up to a fine sheen
on a roll, mellowing out at the tail end
like a sea-bell wrapped in harbour mist.
Her mouth disappears in sunshine.
Words bluster, whisper; a kissed cheek,
a top hat, then she's smaller, diminished
by distance, in a space between daylight's
bare-shoulders. I imagine all the people
she has known. What was his name?
Where did they go? How close you can get
to see-through pink ears, still feel alone
and related. She will see them again
in Spanish cathedrals, night train-windows.

*Dad, come on dad, come on mum – run.*
We fill the spaces between lilies
and thumbs, canada geese that are not
to be touched and two wooden bears
for the children. Leave behind eyes that pour
through wild roses and bright green hearts
on the water: '*Tell us when*'. '*Just smile*'.
Radio news in the tea room: what the bride
is wearing at that other wedding, further
than the far side of the soul. I climb out

of myself, pick my way between gloves
of white lightening, envelopes, marmalade,
a baby crawling on the grass.

This elderly man in a plush weave of cloth
that breathes for him; no sense of concern
at sitting far removed from his children
and their children; staring at the azure sky,
sensing the moment reaching back
to contain these lives, forward
to evening laughter, a river of words
without language, that softens as he walks
in freckled light among the pines.

# Eyewitness

Here they are in dramatis personae:
slack-jaw, blank-stare, pensive as cattle; one,
a bespectacled historian, dictaphone live,
pencil-in-hand, foredoomed to record
the sound of a sailor, wielding a lighter
to knock out a tooth souvenir.

# The Iron Woman

Waiting for the phone to ring in the Miner's Welfare –
the men told last moment of the night's mass-picket:
grabbing coats, thrown about on cratered roads, hands
pressed against the roof as we swerved past haulage yards,
treatment plants, the anthracite air leaking darkness

into ineffable fathoms. Picket of pale smiles, voices
of fiery clouds, the blood in my head cooling, crosswinds
asking if something will happen. I was with Police Watch
organised to observe the policing of pickets, the coppers
were in transits, eyes triggered, fishing-out bits of sandwich

from between their teeth. I saw her cycle towards us
in the early hours  to picket the night shift going in.
Her silhouette softening under fence lights – Women
Against Pit Closures, clapping – to dismount at the gates,
embrace her comrades on the line, time backed into a corner.

She must have been in her eighties. Front row, third left.
Same seat, row, teacher, slate; a spire she can no longer see.
Orchestras, chapel choirs, dance nights at the Greystones.
Her husband's lungs ripping themselves inside-out
on summer nights. Elvis in the Closed Shop taproom: she

danced to Blue Suede Shoes. She's as live to me as the guilt
I feel for trying to escape – not the people – the mining life,
through the promise-lie of education, to stumble upon myself
in a stranger on Collegiate Crescent, speaking a language
that wasn't my own, nor was it his. She carries me home:

coal and a chicken in our handlebar basket. I carry her
in coffee spoons, sleeplessness, a love of nocturnal beasts
that run against the odds. I see her in the childhood of stars,
a spinal canal of grassed-over spoils, words I mine.
Cycling past the pithead baths the miners built themselves,

gutted by vandals. A sculpted half-wheel – *Red Road Radio:*
*Music like it used to be*. A car swerves, beeps its horn,
an old willow uprooted by the storm. Pumping her legs,
riding like dancing. The listed Victorian colliery offices
and clock tower. Her silken feet light on her hips and heart.

# The Six Goodbyes of the Eightfold Path

Can you be finishing off now, my love?
I wonder if I will hear that voice at the end –
Can you be finishing off now, my love?
While I'm pouring soup in a cereal bowl
with the hairline crack, cutting the lawn,
or tap-tapping away in the first floor computer suite
where librarian, Paula calls me, 'my love' –
'Can you be finishing off now, my love?'
As the cursor freezes on the page of a poem
about Miles Davis, 'the choir boy from hell'
who, according to the poet
never wanted to be loved or love,
never wanted to be here. I don't mean 'here',
pouring soup in a cereal bowl
with the hairline crack, cutting the lawn,
or tap-tapping away in the first floor computer suite
where librarian, Paula calls me, 'my love.'
I mean here in moving salt and shirttails,
playing himself out of the world
into the night, trumpeting solos that cut
too deep in self-defeating risk-taking.
Can you be finishing off now, my love?
There is a big-bottomed Bluebottle
on Bob Brighton's paint-soaked blocks
of raw hessian and flax, here,
in the first floor computer suite where we
are welcome to weep and flirt, suffocate
on rags of time, imitate a cockatoo
but are forbidden to shout: *If I find you*
*slept with that witches brew of malice*
*and spite, as god is my witness, Terry,*
*my love, I'll fucking swing for you.*
Can you be finishing off now, my love?

I wonder if I will hear that voice at the end –
Can you be finishing off now, my love?
As I walk through the glass doors of swing
to the entrance hall, children's poetry
on the wall, a tiptoe over discarded chips,
down yellow-trimmed steps
onto the Surrey Street thoroughfare
where light meets the road in beautiful legs,
optical sheets of water. Here, Berry Dazzle,
Mango Tango and *Go Ape* at Quench Food
and Shakes on my left. Glass-housed plants
the dinosaurs ate, in a geological timeframe
at odds with Zooby's Deli. A man shouts:
*Why do drivers stare at me?* Sunflowers,
contorted willow in the scornful florists.
I notice passing drivers are staring at me too.
Wonder if I will hear that voice at the end –
Can you be finishing off now, my love?
As I'm pressing odd tiles, bits of brass
and metal in hope the dryer will fire
in the *Men's* or listening to the litany
of remembrance on the telephone:
*Do you remember Eric?*
*You do remember Eric.*
*You bloody ought to remember Eric,*
*You played football with his two lads*
*Jason and the small'n on the green.*
*You do remember Eric.*
*Jason and Twisty; his two lads.*
*Took them to watch Everton at Goodison,*
*course you remember Eric; his wife*
*worked with your Auntie Doris,*
*and Mabel, Derek's Draper's missus,*
*where they make the Liquorice Allsorts.*
*Course you remember Eric.*
*He wrote to the Liverpool Echo.*
*What you said about the cause*
*of his balding head when he*

*was creosoting the garden shed.*
*He nearly won a dalek on your behalf,*
*for that. Remember, your mother said:*
*'It's not coming in the house.'*
Can you be finishing off now, my love?

I wonder if I will hear that voice at the end –
Can you be finishing off now, my love?
While I'm queuing for a newspaper
that comes with a copy of Black Beauty
or riding the Low Edges bus as it stops
at the lights by the Rhythm and Booze,
when a man says: *I'm on the bus*
and two teenage girls say *fuck* a lot,
on the front seat, each girl in turn, upping-
-the-ante in the repetitive use of the word.
I ask myself if this is the sound of the Higgs
Boson particle. Feel the primordial urge
to invoke passengers to relax the muscles
on either side of the spinal column. Chant
the Six Goodbyes of the Eightfold Path,
slowly at first, hesitant, tentative,
breathing in, two-three-four, and out,
with-a-low-hum, working towards
a quiet growl, breathing like a hidden cave,
stronger, surer, centred-low in the body,
faster, louder, hips swaying, tension
mounting, power reaching its epiphany
at Eric Gilbert Domestic and Commercial
Carpets and Flooring when the top deck
is moving like the pottery and egg
decorators of ancient Machu Picchu.
Can you be finishing off now, my love.

I wonder if I will hear that voice at the end –
Can you be finishing off now, my love?
As I savour the last mouthfuls of slow flame
in the pub with the old schoolhouse tables
and chairs. Listen to how 'she' was older
than Edwin, who wants the band together,
but doesn't know about the bass player
and the rest are quite scary. How 'he'
wants everything to end in a row with Daisy,
'who's got her own thoughts.' Can you
be finishing off now, my love?
The engine boys on the table to my left
talking espionage and motorbikes, agree
*It's sad to die of alcohol but aren't we*
*food for worms?* and *Aren't worms food*
*for birds?* And just when you think we'll
never smile again: *Aren't the birds*
*that fuzzy bit around the edge, aeons*
*hence?* How they nod like the front bench
at question time, make it all sound
so nailed down. Can you be finishing off
now, my love? I find words on a flyleaf
in hues of blue that could chill a butcher's
larder: *I'm caught between light and dark*
*like the dust which needs both to dance.*
I must have written those years ago
but am not sure what they mean. Is it
a reaction against myself ? Do they say
I never wanted to be loved, or love,
never wanted to be here? I don't mean 'here',
in the pub with the old schoolhouse
tables and chairs, drinking the pale horse
that talks of mercy. I mean here
in ocean light and lips of ancient wood,
playing myself-out, in riffs that cut
too deep in self-defeating risk-taking.
Can you be finishing off now, my love?
I breathe-in the resin-scented, rain rinsed

beer-garden air. Say to myself:
*It's the leg room that counts not the seating.*
Raise a glass to the postman who
found Eric, half naked in the side entry,
reading the gas meter. Marvel at our Lady
of Loudness in her screaming pink shift
with student teachers, by the framed map
of Where the Bombs Fell in Sheffield:
*Oh my god, talk about my last night*
*of freedom! I dreamt I was driving the car,*
*we were lost, I took over the wheel*
*on a hill but the handbrake wouldn't work*
*and Sam couldn't drive and we*
*were rolling backwards. I always dream*
*about failing brakes and a face*
*that suddenly appears on the other side*
*of the windshield when I'm on the hill*
*with friends who are wrapping presents*
*but can't drive, and we're rolling back*
*and the face becomes a megaphone;*
*John Lennon with a megaphone,*
*sometimes my Uncle Hughie, and we're*
*rolling backwards, picking up speed*
*and a face appears and that's all I*
*remember before I wake up. Weird innit?*

# Nostalgia for the Light

Sunglasses and bare shoulders,
rapid-fire dialect among the market stalls
on the day the Caravan of Death
came to Calama. A city and commune
of ancient pepper-trees and partridges,
the arched bone of a dancer's foot
and blueberries; wheat, fish and water
in the driest hot desert on earth.

*ni pena ni miedo,* written in the sand
with earthmoving equipment, in letters
so big they can only be read from the air
when threads of volcanic steam clear
and the desert opens its book of memory.

Goat bells, washing lines, motorbikes,
a caesarean section. A painter adding light
to a mouth in the plaza, on the day
a death squad did the bidding of a dictator
regaled by presidents, a prime minister
of Great Britain. *Neither shame nor fear*

inlaid in the desert, read by the stars.
The initial '*n*' with its sweeping downstroke,
windblown sand on the windward edge;
gentle angles, letters that glide and whorl,
working with the desert grain, looping out
of repose so each word remains unbroken.

Women of Calama, numb-blood pulsing,
driving as if in a blizzard, to hospitals,
wasteland and morgues: corridors, offices,
a basement of corpses. On the solitary road
into the desert, mirages and salt lakes –
seamless from the turquoise milk of the sky.
Baptismal snow on the observatory dome.

Astronomers tell us we live behind time;
search beyond the light for our origins
in a sack of atoms in a halo of winter.
In the Atacama's absolute desert, not a blade
of grass or weightless god. Not a gnat, bat
or bowling alley but the women of Calama
search below sand for a scintilla of bone
with a hand-held plastic shovel. Husbands,
sons, brothers – a splinter of guitar finger –
the same calcium galaxies are made of;
pieces of unfinished laughter, a cheek bone
with the bullet lodged in, or something more:
the cellular memory of indigenous wars
lasting three centuries; pre-Columbian signs
of justice and renewal in the sudden light
of a tooth that becomes the entire universe.

If you trace the giant sweep and bend
of the text on the desert's open page –
five minutes to reach the 'i' at an easy pace –
run gently on the ineluctable soft berms,
three-, four-foot high to the next word,
heavy-bodied, giddy-headed,
you smell the white cap snowmelt, hear
the desert breathe lightly, the Milky Way
read softly. As for the poet?

I could say: Raul Zurita.

I could say: the dead that change places
with the living.

You would need to study dust.

# The Laughter of Women

Five minutes from the home of Stockport County. Tannoy words
blur around the edges, apologies for the late running of this
train. Small birds are swirling in the air above a sleep-in of sheep.
I love the way they work the light, inside out, upside down, as if
they're threading seeds in furrows of air and in a sudden switch
of blades, put the valley on its feet. Today, we will meet in Café
Moonstruck Hammock, bounce like loose limes down a walnut
stairway that opens on grained-pine tables and benches. Spoons
and forks will be made of bamboo or bonsai, as will the black-
pepper pot that will remind me of a rolling pin. I'll take off my
watch, shoes, clothes: you will smile. I'll put them back on again.
We will eat black-eyed bean pie and an orange served on a
saucer, segments spooning in two symmetrical lines. You will
rearrange the bones in my right hand. I will feel as serene as a
buddha's cat on St Kilda. Your eyes will bring to mind a peacock-
blue freshwater lake skimmed with mist. The glittering turquoise
splash of a kingfisher. In Oxford Road station, I am walking
towards the laughter of women.

# Ithaca

They've tried to hide it but the kids
have heard the talk. Barbarians are preparing
to buy the slow tempo of the morning;
disused gods are eating cliff eggs
and walnuts in abandoned ice-cream vans.
You've seen a well-dressed, elegant man
asking tourists if they could spare the biscuits
on their saucers and Cassandra with staff
and hurricane hair-do, wandering
between soup halls and a shrine that bubbles
in a tree-lined courtyard – foretelling
of a military coup. People stare at her, buy
postcards as the mad pomegranate tree burns
in the garden of tumultuous poses.

They've tried to hide it but the kids
have heard the talk. Barbarians are preparing
to buy the unruly salted air we breathe;
daily routines in the houses and streets
are open to the highest bidder. You've heard
of the priest driving at police in a gas mask
on his quad bike; the eighty year old woman
who, bathed in petrol, paid for the flames
with a smile of Piaf – refused to be a burden
to her children. Praise the fortitude of suicides:
Dimitris Christoulas, a retired pharmacist,
preferred a bullet in Syntagma Square
to delving deep into garbage heaps for food
after a life-time's work. No one's blaming you.

How near we live to our lives: a sister
who plays the concertina with light brown arms,
a brother who sleeps inside the broken timbers
of voyages, listens to radio commentaries
of Man United in the Champions League;
father, purple chiton clasped at the shoulder,
striding across a vineyard, wild-eyed lions
staring under the dead echo of a cloudless sky.
Do you see them? A numinous orange glow
above the neo-classical picture house
that once featured Charlton Heston in Ben Hur;
now, it's ash drifts like burnt celluloid; closer,
an open-air kitchen: nurses, teachers, clowns
on stilts waving at you by a clouded samovar,
graduates serving tea to graduates, who serve tea.

You bring me back to Ithaca, in jeans
and perfect armour. We hurl down the broken doors
to the sea's orchards, the skies wheat; welcome
the return of outlaw clouds; transform ourselves
on pathways of rain and ruins: younger, stronger
we march beyond pepper trees, tritons,
and the Marble Arch. Later, we will pay
for a cinema seat with a blonde onion.

# Afterlife

After my life I find myself in Dagenham
and Redbridge, forcing entry into Marks
and Spencer's: *This is a giant slice
of cooked ham*, I said, recreating myself
wearing trousers, curing bacon,
translating black smoke rising in circles,
comparing ox-hearts to full-lips,
on the high street, language to the song
of a missal thrush, unkillable laughter
on library steps, the smell of coffee.
That's a bit of thread bare carpet; this,
the smell of vinegarred fish; here's
Sailing Bye before the shipping forecast.

After my life I find myself ascending
on the assisted chin-dip to a bass line
that mangles the brain endings, a blurr
of birdseed lyrics: *You are, you are
reachin' … there's a fire, a fire catchin' …*
Hear Joan of Arc say all bad metaphors
are immortal; the soft roar of swift air,
silence in the buildings, sobbing
of the man inside the burning woman
as if we're never, merely, who we are.
What do you think of that, Mr Death?

Is the one who was once me
The Singing Molecatcher of Pig Island?
I'm spending my death in Large Print
Romance: spines of silent talking books,
the click of a purse clasp, a faint scent
of urine, laughter and voices
that must have a source. This, the room
where souls seek the bodies they crave:
a librarian's gypsum fingers, shelving
Love in Stormcrow Castle; Mrs Green
of Fishamble Street, retaining water
and an albino vampire on a vinyl sofa.
Don't take me completely: don't leave me!

After my life I returned to the woman
who used to serve but now she drinks
in the Sheaf View Inn; lives with a cocker
spaniel, a bichon frise and a man.
I find myself noticing small details:
the earth accelerates, passes onions, oranges,
scaffolding; meets oncoming streaks
of pale-blue gold in the surface water.
I'm in love with movement: greens, ambers,
Love and Sandwiches, Cakes and Steel,
bridge walls that sweat oil and ochres,
people whose stare returns to itself through
bus-lit reflections of a stranger; cantaloupes,
betting shops, baths on the side walk;
the woman beside me, smiling as she talks
for the unseen fox and neighbourhood stars,
living for a second time.

# How Long?

As long as a slab of hard wood is a dining table,
makeshift bed and air-raid shelter, for people
who can't plan more than two hours in advance.
As long as women ask who is present for breakfast,
who is absent and why? As long as strike jets
patch-quilt the sky and refugees pass through the sun,
eyes swimming. As long as a Grandfather clock
cannot compete with the bulldozer's teeth.
As long as a gate and petrified sapling
are all that remain standing. Who will find doors
for the handles? As long as rifle-eyes buttonhole hips
and hair for a single spray of rose with thistle heads
in the olive groves. As long as reed flutes cry
in butterfly-dark alleyways, where laughter rubs
its eyes over dance steps that go wrong.
As long as people marry, depart and return
in the night. As long as the teachers award prizes
for stories written about a zoo on the other side
of the border where children of the Intifada,
under cover of the lemon arbour, journey catlike
to feed the giraffe and zebra. As long as dead soldiers
are called 'non-operative personnel' and bookshops
fence firearms. As long as a bubble pipe is no match
for the corrugated solidity of a General's moustache.
As long as a stranger offers dried fruit to a woman
with child in a stationary train between checkpoints.

# Chute

Sixty-inch screens
from two-room flats,
old beliefs,
        lino scraps,
chicken legs from
behind the moon,
piling-up inside
            the skips
that line our streets.

That fricative hiss
in a scaffold chute –
ghost bricks,
        bar codes,
    bed-time stories,
air-blade dryers,
in shop-sealed wrappers,
        a gorilla mask.

What they take off
            your thigh
can be put in your face.
I have no throat
and I must rage against
directional arrows
on cardboard boxes.
        That sound
of pruning shears,
discouraging words
in a corridor
        of ankle high hot
grey pipes.

Coins and fingers
in a sofa, dumped
for a 'corner'
        with chrome feet
and pouffe.


        Greedy doors
are angled steep
to raise skip sides
            take more in.
Wobbly bubbly glass,
a set of sash windows,
a flash wind
from Graves Park,
cathode-ray lit curtains,
the Maltese Falcon.


The first time ever I saw your skip
I lean inside, a hand appears,
we dance with a third eye
and a chair that likes poetry
when its legs are in the air.


A dog that dreams of a church wall
that's long gone, raises
a hind leg at the yellow metal base.
I don't want to be cremated…
just scattered between greedy doors
        angled steep


    a Christmas tree
        in monsoon rain,
an errant eye lash
    on a damp mattress
'I told you':
        'You told me –
    I told you! '

The neighbour
  calling my name
    while nodding
      at his
        stylish car
  like a dashboard dog.

  A white ram
    tied to a stake,
      the girl prepared
  to accept her fate.
    Henry the Hoover.

I read of Hephaestus, beater
of the cuirass and greaves.
His mother threw him out of heaven
for making plastic windows.

They still sell tripe on London Road;
I dream awake in the barbers
of pigs turning back into people.

# Dark Matter

When the fence is repaired at one end
it is shattered by the wind at the other.
The front door's glottal stop off-beat
like my neighbour's hammer glancing
headless nails. He's taken to prising
bricks into the gaps, throwing the debris
on my side. As the earth mis-shapes
under the weight of shoppers and skips,
we seem, more than ever divided
and alone. Insurrections of branches
ring voices from the birdless dark, wind
tugging at the moorings of the house;
rain tapping like a vintage Olivetti
on the window sill. I open the door

offer to help the man who loves a fence,
blowback pressing on the cheeks
of my face; he's falling out of his wind-
tricked shadow like Ajax on the down
swing slicing through a solitary eye,
lopping off a monstrous tail, lying
in the glassy slag of blood and skin
that was his herd. I wake in the belly

of a dream: bust up fence float, aside
clothes pegs and Seneca's Tragedies.
My neighbour, living his reality
TV fantasy, doing the Mexican wave
with his toes and this week started quiet.
We light a small fire, a signal intended
for Neighbourhood Watch or a spinney
of galaxies shaking their buds, telling us
who we are, where we're from or
something profound. The wind has left
a double page of signs in a thin coating

of snow, together with trees, houses
in the same order as before. The fence

is an exploded view: *Wind kill in Limbo*
by Cornelia Parker. Will it come together
again? Or resume its disorderly tropos –
matter into light, pulp to comic strip
of the Road Runner unflattening himself,
re-joining the chase of his mirrored twin
at the speed of the Road Runner squared.

Hydraulic arms and chains take the strain
in his driveway. In Our Time radio talk
of Xerxes, vibrating with anger:
men beheaded, the Hellespont lashed
and branded, redress for his storm-
wrecked bridges as the blown mist
recovers its laughter at the water's edge.
I make peace with rotten wood
bearing traces of age-old knots;
white bed sheets and hands fly from
a plastic basket. Hear knives of rain
from gutters stab as I put the squeeze
on a teabag in a leaking cup. Compose:

   *Help – Shed wanted. Ten by*
  *Eight (or slightly larger).*

   *Must be tongue-in-groove*
  *for scattergun apple tree orchard.*

# Litany

Because you made me pulsate
like hot peach trees, reel like liquid skies
the colour of naked limbs. Because you were
the rain that dreams of larkspur
and woodruff, the smell of loam and bubble-
gum laughter as the pub door opened.
Because we felt the same way about the city
of leaves and the miners' strike, string-vests
and washing lines in back yards. Was it Neruda
who said love is a three-legged dance
on a reclaimed staircase with two right turns?
I loved you as a seasoned stockpile
of 3´ by 4´ adores the sun. You said love
is what happens when you feel the ocean's
clamour prime your heart, when the roots
of larch and birch nourish your fingers
and toes and you see the world anew. It's true,
when we first met my senses were alert
to amber clouds radiant like hives, the smell
of the bread bin, burl in the bark, iron
in the dew; it's true, when we first met, I did
see the world anew. Was it Hegley who said,
love is a scream in the bathroom?
Remember, we debated what it meant to say
space or spruce is 'real' compared
to love's laughing grief. We agreed real
is Yorkshire puddings, stilton evenings
but when we talked of Plato's cave,
prisoners blinking in the crackling air
where one shadow may hide another, we were
no longer sure. When we recited Neruda,
I loved you as rivers foam to the song
of whitethroats. Here, I loved you as burglars
escaped through the cellar while managers
ate a steak dinner; here, in this pub we

called the '197,' I loved you like tomatoes
long to bounce down stepping stones,
passing kipper sheds and jagged rocks
to the monumental jaw bone of a whale; here,
at this table under the caped silhouette
of the Porto Sandeman, as folk musicians
played button accordian. Remember, we
didn't know what a euphonium was, so we
bought another round of drinks, quoted
Marx from *The Class Struggles in France*,
asked whose side Christ was on, and why all
the greats wore clinically intriguing volumes
of hair. Here, under the caped silhouette
of the Porto Sandeman, we debated
what it means to know that string quartets
and the sans-culottes are real
compared to amour. We agreed love happens
on Ward 53. We agreed love happens
in Peru and the Bungalows and Bears
on the Cantril Farm estate where Maggie Kelly
bought me a chilli, asked if I threw
that tennis game in the hospital grounds.
We agreed love happens at the Showroom
on the big screen in *The Crying Game*.
That night your chrome yellow Mini-cooper
went missing outside the Star and Garter;
remember, we walked in donkey jackets
by the burnt-out boathouse, a glycerine lake
under the alopecia moon. I called you *three
birds that teach three birds to sing.*
I called you *The Burning blue breaks
of the sea.* Your navel was an ear
to the shore – the bark of silence. Now,
I throw you a bone. How could I forget
your cold-war tantrums and bonfire eyes
Niagara could not quench. How could I forget
Your six quavers of silence to the apocalypse
smile and when we talked of Plato's cave,

where the shadow-mimes signify and prisoners
second guess, we knew it was war.
When we talked of the missing four weeks
we agreed we were déjà vu and amnesia
in the same conversation. Tell me everything
you know about Medusa, Cruella De Vil,
Ivor Cutler. Because you were a tyrannacide
hiding behind another tyrannacide, disguised
as a florest. Because I couldn't forget
the rocket-salad, free range eggs you launched
from the kitchen hatch. Was it Bukowski who
said love is a lot of bad movies, and a hair pin
in the ass? Because I didn't fear your assassin
who stabbed me in the arm with an Easter egg.
I feared waiting between Everyday Loans and
Noble Amusements for the cab-door's yawn,
that *How-funny-you-are* smile. I feared a spine
of burning salt and billowing lace at dawn.
I feared waiting between Everyday Loans and
Noble Amusements for *Three birds to teach
three birds to sing.*

# Flood

Rain

Rain in Sheffield falls on *Jazz*
*at the Lescar*
on the anarchist tree surgeons
of Heeley Green
on the Abbeydale Picture House
car-booted into perpetual revival,
in baths for sale up to the brink
on London Road.

Rain falls on five young girls
sitting on a wall, wet as waves
drifted towards the lifted ocean,
singing that Weather Girl's hit.

*Oh I'd say – if someone else –*
*I'd say: Why did you do that?*
*You can't begin – traffic lights*
*under water, two months pregnant –*
*I go in, buy my Gorillaz album,*
*New Timberland boots on.*

Can anyone help several men
scaling a wall off Brightside Lane,
a fern tub, car and oil drum
borne on the tidal ruck below?

*You always look, check the level,*
*the banks near the bridge,*
*that pub. Seven months later*
*I gave birth to a carp.*

Rain falls on librarian Kath
in a Reykjavik hotel room,
her Hillsborough home half
submerged on the TV news.

Rain falls on a one-time Lumberjill
of the timber corps, who cut down
trees while the men were at war.
Between rescue workers, her hands
hold hands, the safety-cord lifted,
her ankles dissolve as she wades,
flaccid knees like belisha beacons
peering across the water surface,
her frozen smile between shores.

Rain falls on the self-pouring tea pot
of 1866. Rain falls
on outsourcing and cheap imports,
on a long dance hall –
a salsa class at the workers club
on Mulehouse Road.

## II

Bow waves above the knee
water on the bus ankle-deep,
clouds piled high like rubble.
A woman sitting on the top deck
listening to the rain's church Latin
rinsed with Anglo-Saxon, verse
of Nether Edge, Manor Park,
Heeley Green, Walkey library,
anti-phonics from helicopters,
air-lifting workers who rise
as if from themselves, water
submerging a reception desk.
*My son was at King Edwards.*
*That boy's sister was in his class –*
*my son knew his sister.*

## III

Parents marooned in the undawned
Outdoors and Gardens – dark aisles
of a do-it-yourself store, searching
for sun loungers, picnic blankets,
to stumble upon their inner-child
between multi-purpose roof adhesive
and the night's dream self. Eye full
of dalek, Marineville and Titan,
descending in unblind enchantment,
a glimmer of power tools, Troy and
Phones of the World Security Patrol
with Marina – cursed to silence
or another would die – to the rescue
of a ransomed under-water world
with every happy wound. *Stingray,*
*Stingray,* multi-reflecting trolleys,
ripples of neon signage, beaneries,
pharmacies, florists. Sheffield rose
from the water, magnified by a rain
drop rocked-still on plate glass.


## IV

Rain

You could hear it breathing, behind
barricades, gathering itself to fall
elsewhere, then everywhere else,
without tears, a clock ticking, water
lapping in *Mrs Bouquets* – Claire up
to her knees, sunflowers, car keys,
daughter, Georgia, ten, camera shy.

*I was so high on her list.* Rain falls
on Christine whose friend, Debbie,

survived the flood and a brief time
afterwards. *I was one of the four
she left letters to*: 'My wonderful
no nonsense down-to-earth friend –
until you'd had a few drinks!
Buy yourself something frivolous'.
*I was so high on her list.*

V

Flighty rhythms, fitting, cross-
threading, a blot of blue above
the yard where alarms wail
as cars dry out, doors fly open,
insurance assessors on the way
to the garage on the hill.

The sun drenches the rain's cheek,
the sky colours us in
with the body's memory, roses
grow in skips on Penistone Road.

Mechanical limbs are liberated
in impromptu bits of dance
to Mambo No 5 and We are Family
along the assembly line.

A model ocean-going liner
drifts towards the elevator
in a warehouse and retail Atlantis.
Matt glances over his shoulder
as he works the flagstoned patio,
listening through Judith's stare
from inside her conservatory door:
*Keep sweeping*! *Keep sweeping*!

## Host Rufus Regardless Addresses the Artists at Dr Sketchy's

Draw her from beneath the skin
as if you're in the gaps between
muscles and magnesium flashes
that match the mood of bright salt,
lactic acids in her fluid limbs.

Is that an artist's shadow
on your picture plane or a someone
keeping the pencil moving?
You're thinking, this isn't art –
cami-knickers and research
for a slow fan-dance  with glitter-
bowel and stripper's-knee –
it's difficult to lie with integrity.
Nobody's asking you to.

Draw from the laughter of cells
in each nerve to the ache
of her smile. Next time Gilda Lilly.
Is the mask under her face
or the other way round. Whisky Falls.

Skin is an open border to the epoch
inside, where you encounter
the journey of blood as she dances
on the verge of dawn, inside
each mark you make. Muddy Rumours.

Don't rein her in, she'll make swings
of your hair. Fasten on to the scent,
shoulder blade to the diagonal hip,
liquid lines as she transfers weight…
cut her loose, try again.
Look for that dissolving smile, fear
of being found between resistance
and release. Does knowing her more
mean drawing her clothes back on?
That Babel's Tower of stacked chairs
framing her turn – block it in.

If you're feeling tense – Raw Ghost
is now on tap at 6.4 %  Put your feet
up, lie on the sea-bed of near coma.
Listen to the swish of charcoal,
the squeak and crack of the unsayable.
Is that a train overhead or acoustics
on a loop for effect? Remember,
the marks we don't make
are our spaces, unparalysed by fact.
Please – thank your artiste Joan
of Speke for her cross-dress routine.

# Classically Trained

He's been seen wearing exquisite rags from the Lost and Found,
a kettle of leaves and mumbles. He once wore an Elvis suit
at an embassy dinner. Medicated courtesans were flown in
by *Jet Star*. 'Blueberry', the depressed ballerina
from the New York Met. That Thai masseuse they found dead
in the Paris Hilton: his private number like stigmata on her tan.
Oh, he has the people's blood on his sundial, for sure.
Those intelligence dossiers in western sideboards,
next to crosswords and jigsaws. He's as guilty as old Salah.
After all, there's no smoke without ballistic-missile-systems.

In the beginning he tackled the shortfall in camels and dreams.
kissed ten babies and put out the sun. Restored the fish supper
and typewriter. No end of fun was to be had in the tearooms.
Then his ideas began to explode in the high streets and tramcars.
People bled in the barbers. Surgeons ran out of arms and legs.
Horses lay like broken saddles on the edge of smoking cities.
No one could find the weapons of mass amnesia.
I'm the same with theatre tickets when the play is weeks away.
He forgot where he'd left them. Remember the days of triumph?
He wore the People's thin cotton black pyjama garb.
His moustache was a panther's silence. His stallion, a silhouette.
He said politics is the minted breath of a patron saint,
a hand that holds a fountain pen. Walmart in Madagascar,
star-spangled hunger. He was never known to kill anyone
with a good supply of fingernails. A rice field worker
saw him reading Homer in a rickshaw as enemy tanks
flattened the gates. The press said it was one of 'The Doubles'.
They employ 26 classically-trained actors. It's the only role
they play. He's a difficult man to sum up.

When I saw him he looked like a man pouring tea from a flask
in the glare of footlights as he waited for the din to die down.

# Permit

Do the eggs in the fridge need a permit? Where
neither the dead die nor the living live,
without passing three road blocks and five checkpoints
between Tulkarm and Ramallah.

What questions do those who return ask strangers,
to whom they themselves are strangers?
Is the small woman who lived next door smaller still?
Does the centuries-old fig tree still stammer at odd times?

Where the fruit in a bowl forms a parliament
when elders return from weddings and mortuaries.
Does the barber still dance tango with a matador's countenance
in the tea house when business is slow?

Where kids kick a ball between crater and curfew,
argue over a goal and the girl with the mango-sad eyes,
who wanted to play. Do rivers surrounded by poems
and lips need a permit to reflect Red Gazelles?

Where the girl who wanted to play, cycled
by the checkpoint and a soldier chased her and a dog
chased the soldier. The dog's face is on the wall too.
Does the orange-tufted sunbird need a permit?

# In Search of Yellow House Lane

They remind themselves that life is short. A Spanish voice –
sounding like a full ashtray at 3am – on a loop
in the lounge. Lips on skin earn their skin. Fireworks –
ten days from Fright Night. That's how it begins. His collar bone,

her weightlessness, shadows bigger than their own bigness
on the wall, an eyebrow for a cheek bone, ribs like sandbars
working Southport's shoreline. She is Joan of Arc ablaze,
headlights – a waterless wave returning them
breathless to spines of books, underwear, an open drawer.

When they face each other, for they do face each other,
she can hear the coastal breakers detonate in his kneecap;
nets of darkness disturb her breasts in a hollowed-out whelk shell
of pelvis and hips. She laughs at laughter: a sea within a sea,

his fragile head, an unfired pot. She circles the Weetabix.
Marmalade and metaphysics, a funhouse face underside
of a teaspoon. How will they live in separate exiles
of multi-storey fibreglass with piebald trees in parking lots

after this? He asks her about the prostate gland. She talks of Tao:
the Watercourse Way. They walk the bouncing planks, pass
lifebelts, the Model Railway, the narratives of the Heritage Café,
to that place where what has happened hasn't happened yet.

# Do I Still Exist If You Don't See Me?

*for Francesca Woodman*


She slips inside her skin
behind the flowered paper
her grey silhouette window-lit.

How the sun must warm her back.
She takes a finger-grip
rips-off the head at the chin,

disembowels herself with light.
Who was the first to erase
the other? That just-breath summer,

when she faded ghost-like
into bare walls and floorboards,
as if the lens's long exposure

could return her to wood and stone,
resist even death as her ceiling
dripped monochrome celluloid.

*Bunny Hun, I 'm in the photo cave.*
*Text me if the moon rocks*
*should strike you.* She can't recall

his face, her stolen cycle, hesitates
above the neon veins of Manhattan,
clothes-lines on hot asphalt roofs,

a foot poised, stepping through her
own motion. Smudged
by a nape of salt rain, a sill of cats.

On both sides of the camera now
undressing in one winding spiral
like she used to peel an orange

so she can furl herself together later
around him as he sleeps
knowing that if he wakes

before she becomes whole, she dies,
the sun-fried window,
white on white.

# Oak

Outreaching the strangled light, bound
for the island of roots that are wings,
my main limb like a whole tree
hovering above creatures on their road
to where? A blur of fowl detonates
the surface silence, my beard tremulous
in the pond's sky-dream.
I am Jehovah of the acorn, host of lace lice,
star moult, hairy-legged shuddering.
I milk the sun of centuries,
process gases by personal chemistry.
Separate from the earth, I marvel
their movement, spray-on leggings, fit bits.
Slowdown – I want to say – you host
your own ghosts? I love, I drink
my strangeness in all-year-round words.
That crackclick's my arthritic neck,
but enough of me, they're young clouds
with no final shape. Fake sadness,
real sadness, knuckle jointed, bottle-
butted, hollowed out underneath.
Taproots tug at my crown. *Oh-my-god*
laughter, ivy-spun halters, a grey bird sleeks.
I am the comprehending cycle,
hair down to my liquid waist,
roots fuse, give, take, dig deep to stop
the earth from sinking like a tongue
down the throat of the unknown.
I am: what am I? Palate of new-born blue,
coffee, cask and leather brown,
chlorophyll, bleached grey under
a wooden bench in loving memory.
A child's boot, my shadow on a face,
I'm falling from the page.
Midges loop back on themselves, write

on their writing. Rhododendron
flowers, upside down at island's edge,
undulating faces – brothers, sisters
of truculent gods. Red plastic hearts
on Rustlings Road, dragonflies batting
on a pediment. Words from my canopy.

# Memoir

At my parents, Christmas, I looked
for that boy where I no longer exist.
Key, still in the yellow backdoor,
smell of wet dog by the fridge,
not knowing where I was til I heard
the orange, Wembley football,
thudding on house, garden wall,
saw kids wrestle one another's hearts
for a goal scoring chance, climb
their own spines to head a high cross.

Man-o-war masts of smog – gilded
by sodium, torn on aerials – unfurling
the ship's prow figure-head
of Brenda Scoefield, pedalling into low
definition silhouette, her grimace
set in millstone; handlebar basket
full of mincemeat. A kid on his knees
spine flexing, retrieving the ball
from under a car like a beggar's dog.

I escaped, died, went to Fazakerely,
leaving behind elbows of mist,
foreheads of salt, spaces for others
to inhabit, a street you cannot leave.
At my parents, Christmas, I looked
for that boy where I no longer exist.
Falling down, getting up, hard to see
for eye-scalding sweat, a shoe flying
overhead, detonated laughter muted
in the sulphurous haze. 'One-two', off

a gate stump, a cheeky nutmeg
by the coal truck, a rolling barrel
of scuffs, charges, kicks and curses
several feet from disturbing the peace
in every directionless riot of travel.
A kettle boils, the acousmatic voice
of the apocalypse, Big Dora, boom-
clang-squeaking like a boxcar axle
pledging an imminent reckoning
for the price of bacon bones, five
Woodbine and the Wembley ball's
thunder-clap on her window pane.

How many of 'me' are there?
One, of oak-moss smeared denim,
white milk below the bough's skin,
swinging on a fraying rope, shaking
stiffness out of branches. One,
of the swishy hips-first walk
and take-the-piss upper-crust drawl
and lisp. One, lying in hiding
on the washhouse, staring
at celestial insect-bites of light.
One, is my brother needing help
with his reading and writing.
My penance is a house of books.

One, of cathode glow, theme tune:
*This is Your Life, Till Death Us
Do Part*, charge of the clothes props
in the garden. *World in Action*, that
naked man with the opening credits.
One, of borderless nature's apples.
What was his name? Stopped cars,
the night train's one-tone treble,
iron-on-iron, spear-on-shield, faint,
building, louder…as in *Zulu*,
echoing across the golf links, other
side of the line. Where do they go?
Do they live in another street
after this one. Who calls them in
at night. Do they return as people
who see themselves as absent?

Under a lamppost a couple arm-
in-arm, the girl's smile-inside
or is it a runnel of vapour, a tear?
Cold pinching her thighs, ears,
from behind, his small red light,
she checks her stride not knowing
that what she does next as the ball
bounces towards her, will resonate
in the questions she asks the men
she meets, the way she sweeps lint
from her nylon stocking, sitting
cross-legged on a bus, kids playing
up. Walks past a wall with a cane.

At my parents, Christmas, mum
told me: *He doesn't speak to her…*
*She doesn't speak to him… neither*
*of them speak to the one upstairs.*
*He's pouring concrete in Australia,*
*she's moved in with a fella – he's*
*not well, it's a bugger and 'Slim'*
*the decorator's gone,* recalls him
drying his socks on a blow lamp.
Mrs Livesley, *harmless enough*
swinging her cotton-string mop
cleaning her lamp-post out front
all she is into the act, declaiming
into the gums of the wind:
*Don't think ah don't bloody know*
*what yah sayin' 't' other side*
*of curtains 'cause ah bloody do.*

All that was four decades ago.
The years, trailing one another
like novice spies at first,
then highway robbers, galloping
alongside, getting a grip. People
long gone. One, fathered a child,
got that illness we don't mention.
One, threw herself under a train,
smiled as she put out the empties.
Some of cancer, of drink, of time
which is a fog-bound street from
another point of view. Actually,
all that was an hour ago.
Can't see them now for shadows
that self-divide and re-converge,
gaps between the living and dead
we pour through, finding our own
shape, guided by sibilant echoes,
distances, the glimmer of a cheek.
Like lungs of air we cannot hold
on to them for long.

I would run to these kids
playfighting like mountain cubs,
ask them whose side I'm on.
Outnumbered by their own ghosts,
inseparable from sea smoke
out running the wind, oblivious
to the murmured vespers
of other roads, not caring
which side-street of knock-about
they are born or die on, too busy
twisting blood on the ball,
setting fire to their lives
to heed the rat run's engines
as the centuries begin.

# This Lightening Never Ends

*for Miguel Hernandez*

How you couldn't write for the people unless you were with them.
Mouthfuls of sun from the raw-knuckled foothills; ballads of milk
you learned with your ear to the she-goat. How for you – work,
love and water, were a fig tree in a field.

Blood rose like a hood to darken the wind: rhythms of heart's fists,
angry balls and lightening teeth of the gored bull's soliloquy,
volcanically snorted for the low-lamp houses, gangrenous trenches
and in damp columns of prison air, you tried to dream with rats
in your hair. Bring poetry to me in the blood of onions. Defender

of laughter and wounds that spill like inkwells on hushed trains.
Show me how to lower roots that seek the heart with no master
in the shipwrecked flower beds and widowed balconies of Spain;
climb two trees and whistle two nightingales for Miguel Hernandez.

# Meeting Karl Marx in the Sheaf View

I see you walk through the door
Jehovah bearded
minutes before pumps-off,
an Airedale scuffling
from under a table
to snap at your boot lace
as you march past the Tory rags
on the paper stand.

Pints, shorts, shouts: dices
clatter, rocket laughter
bangs on the table, talk
of double-dip, a finger
shattered between barrels,
an own goal on Match of the Day,
your frockcoat buttons
in the wrong eyelets
as you order a drink at the bar.

I want to ask you about being alone,
besieged in your study
by bills from the butchers,
the apothecary, a table
covered with oil cloth, manuscripts,
cups with chipped rims,
two volumed door stoppers
and three legged chairs,
the one with four for visitors.

# There Will Be No Miracles Here

The city is dripping
cameras, my pocket
is damp with ink,
I taste it on my mouth.
Trees smeared
with October's blood
in the gardens
on Princess Street.
A leg in the air, a mouth
gaping, an upturned
beard on the rope climb
under the eyelets
of Edinburgh's castle.
*Health Survival*
*of the Fittest*, ten years
old, one contestant
tears out a kidney
and eats it. Winners i.e.
everyone is awarded
a free photo memento
and a bag full of stones.
Shoppers on pavements
glance into the gardens
at muddied torsos,
faces twisted, inhaling
in agony and foot-slog it
to M & S or s & m.

Words wear a blue dress
swing an axe, poison
an innocent girl, stagger
naked along Rose Street
past the Kenilworth Inn
barrell into Milnes Bar,
the 'Little Kremlin'

looking for Stella… up
Midlothian Road finding
neon lips and thighs,
hollows of collar bones,
describe desire
and the voice
of a broken axle
at the crossroads:
*fuck yah … thank yah 'n'*
*fuck yah,* picking up
a rhythm, belonging
to an unmade hammock
of a man, swaying
before oncoming traffic
inviting drivers to cross
themselves, levitate,
plough into the Cameo
where they're showing
*I Daniel Blake*
*The Girl on the Train*
*Eight Days a Week*
and on the Meadows

a new poem is born
purple and trembling
at busker's junction.
Women in lyrca and fit
– bits jog while pushing
their strollers. Men,
with knees bent, spines
straight, arms extended,
touching one another
and a tree whose boughs
clutch the trunk
lest it burst into laughter.
A pigeon lands bearing
the soul of Queen Mary.
Shoeless singing, candle-

lit in a Spanish accent:
Leonard's *Hallelujah*,
under pointillist canopy
of pancake leaves from
chestnut trees
falling on a hard curve
of forehead, as if cures
to an excess of knowing.

On the next page
the Codfather Chip shop
and Summerhouse minus
its horse sculpture facade
that resembled
a classroom drifting
in a most peculiar way.
It's now the b-side
of a vinyl record
the balanced off-balance
of the unmarked day.
In Blackett Lane
that lone cat sits
like a cold flame,
offering no explanations,
knowing the limits
of her necessity.

# Untitled

*after Keith Piper*

His cheeks are the furrowed earth
and his lips are the patience of endless rain
and his soldier's face is a mother's heart

and his bones are everywhere you dig
and his hair is lush grass rising like incense
and his street smells of pomegranate, bread

and napalm wafting in on fits of wind
and his straw is three rooms and a hammock
that leaps in tunnels that quake

and his leaves are bitter, his roots are sweet
and his pulse is the beat of pagoda bells
one thousand thoughts in the banana groves

and his river bank is her long leg, the hand
they found, the torch she shone
to save the convoy and his tears are stars

her watch and canvass shoe in a ration box
and his silence is the whump-whump,
whump-whump of a helicopter gunship

the size of a mosquito in his field of vision
and his distance is the tenth of a second
his eye lids close – open

# Notes

*Orgreave Mass Picnic*
Written after attending the Orgreave Mass Picnic & Festival on
the 30 year anniversary of the 'Battle of Orgreave'. The festival
celebrated the struggle of mining communities to protect their
livelihood and way of life during and after the year-long miners'
strike of 1984-1985. The festival took place at Catcliffe recreation
ground near the site of the Orgreave coke depot outside
Rotherham in South Yorkshire where the 'battle' took place. I
noticed there was nothing physical on the landscape left to
'place' the events of June 1984 for passers-by or visitors to the
area now an executive housing estate built by Barratt Homes.

*Picasso's Bull*
Inspired by Picasso's suite of eleven lithographs that have been
presented as a master class in how to develop an art work.
Picasso was quoted as saying: *A picture used to be a sum of
additions. In my case a picture is a sum of destruction. I do a
picture – then I destroy it. In the end, though, nothing is lost: the
red I took away from one place turns up somewhere else.* ('Picasso
on Art' edited by Dore Ashton: DA Capo Press New York 1972)'.
In the series of images, all pulled from the same stone, the artist
visually dissects the bull, apparently, to discover its essential
presence from analyses viz the unlayering of its form. Each plate
is a progressive stage in the investigation moving from the
substantive to formal, concrete to abstract. Lithography as a
medium allowed for addition and subtraction from the image
with relative ease.

*Niobe of Gaza*
'Banksy' undertook a tour of Gaza following Israel's attack on
the city in 2014. He left a series of characteristic works on
bombed-out buildings, walls and a door left standing in the
ruins of what had been a house. The image painted on the door
was of Niobe the Greek goddess mourning the murders of her
children as punishment for her pride. Apollo killed all her sons

and Artemis killed all her daughters. Niobe went back to her Phrygian home, where she was turned into a rock on Mount Sipylus (Yamanlar Daðý, northeast of Izmir, Tur.), which continues to weep when the snow melts above it. The image became the subject of a legal controversy over ownership. The owner of the house, Mr. Dardouna, sold the door to a local art dealer, Mr. Belal Khaled, not knowing the value of the work. It was the myth and the image left on the door that inspired *Niobe of Gaza*.

*The Iron Woman*
During the miners' strike I worked with 'Sheffield Police Watch'. This work amounted to standing near or on NUM picket lines acting as witnesses in hope that our presence and recording of events would make police brutality and violence less likely. For the most part we ended up standing with the pickets. On one occasion in the early hours in sub-zero temperatures, I saw an elderly women cycle to the picket line; she must have been in her eighties. I was told by pickets that the men in her family, past and present, had all worked down the mine and that she cycled to the picket line in all weather, each day without fail, to support the striking miners. I don't know her name.

*Nostalgia for the Light*
Written in response to the documentary of the same title released in 2010 by Patricio Guzman to address the lasting impacts of Augusto Pinochet's dictatorship. Guzmán focuses on the similarities between astronomers researching humanity's past in an astronomical sense and the struggle of many Chilean families who still search, after decades, for the remains of their relatives executed during the dictatorship. The documentary includes interviews and commentary from some of the Chilean people affected and from astronomers and archeologists.

*Flood*
On 25 June 2007, the city of Sheffield suffered extensive damage as the River Don broke its banks causing widespread flooding in the Don Valley area of the city. Workers had to be air-lifted

to safety in Brightside. The entire ground floor of Meadowhall shopping centre was submerged. Hillsborough football stadium stood in six feet of water, people scaled walls to escape fast moving water, floating cars and other debris. There were similar scenes in Rotherham, where entire housing estates were inundated with flood waters. The most tragic incident was the death of 13-year-old Ryan Parry. The teenager fell into a swollen river when he took a shortcut through Millhouses Park. I wrote a poem about the flood in 2007 and re-worked it in 2015 with the help of Sheffield people's recollections of that day

### Do I Still Exist If You Don't See Me?
Francesca Stern Woodman (3 April 1958 – 19 January 1981) was an American photographer best known for her black and white pictures of herself or female models. Her images were created using a slow shutter-speed; the long exposure meant movements was captured but appeared as a blur. The effect is curious, as though the camera has been left in a haunted house. Francesca's interest in the female body's movement and becoming in its physical surrounds, together with her talent for composition are essential features of her work. Some have compared her to Surrealist photographers such as Man Ray, others insist she was a feminist, exploring the ways women are pressured to conceal and disguise their true selves. Her work continues to be the subject of great critical acclaim and attention, years after she killed herself at the age of 22, in 1981.

### Oak
Written in response to *Urban Forest's new poetry commissions* and a promenade performance in Endcliffe Park as part of the 2016 Folk Festival in Sheffield.

### Untitled
A response to the painting, 'Untitled' by Keith Piper, a close-up of a warrior's face painted in red emulsion, with dark, vertical stripes tapering down to the chin. The warrior is looking-out, impassively, beyond a U.S. gunship, (flying in front of the face) to engage the eyes of the viewer.

*This Lightening Never Ends*
Miguel Hernandez wrote viscerally about the tragedy and hope he witnessed before and during Spain's civil war. The self-educated, shepherd poet fought on the Republican side. Imprisoned in several of Franco's jails, he continued to write until his death from untreated tuberculosis on 28 March 1942, at the age of thirty-one.